⊞ WE WOULD TAKE THAT DESPISED
OUTCAST OF THE BUILDING
INDUSTRY—THE CONCRETE BLOCK—
OUT FROM UNDERFOOT OR FROM
THE GUTTER—FIND A HITHERTO
UNSUSPECTED SOUL IN IT—MAKE
IT LIVE AS A THING OF BEAUTY—
TEXTURED LIKE THE TREES. ⊞

—FRANK LLOYD WRIGHT
"AN AUTOBIOGRAPHY," 1932

FRANK LLOYD WRIGHT'S
CALIFORNIA HOUSES

⊞   C A R L A   L I N D   ⊞

A N   A R C H E T Y P E   P R E S S   B O O K

POMEGRANATE ARTBOOKS, SAN FRANCISCO

Library of Congress Cataloging-in-Publication Data

Lind, Carla.

Frank Lloyd Wright's California houses / Carla Lind.

    p.   cm.   — (Wright at a glance)

"An Archetype Press book."

Includes bibliographical references.

ISBN 0-7649-0013-7 (hc)

1. Wright, Frank Lloyd, 1867–1959 — Criticism and interpretation. 2. Dwellings—California. 3. Organic architecture — California. I. Title. II. Series: Lind, Carla. Wright at a glance.

NA7235.C2L48 1996   96-18140

728'.372'092—dc20   CIP

Published by

Pomegranate Artbooks

Box 6099, Rohnert Park,

California 94927-6099

Catalogue no. A858

Produced by Archetype Press, Inc.

Washington, D.C.

Project Director: Diane Maddex

Editorial Assistants:

Gretchen Smith Mui and Kristi Flis

Designer: Robert L. Wiser

10 9 8 7 6 5 4 3 2 1

Printed in Singapore

Opening photographs: Page 1: Frank Lloyd Wright about 1916. Page 2: Ennis house (1923), Los Angeles. Pages 6–7: Hollyhock house (1921), Hollywood.

CONTENTS

FROM 1917 TO 1927 FRANK LLOYD WRIGHT (1867–1959) flirted with glamorous California, hoping to gain an architectural foothold in its rapidly developing economy. He designed only six houses in America in this decade, five of which were built in the Los Angeles area—work that Wright musically called his "romanza," or romance. Despite personal and professional troubles, he was able to apply his vision of an indigenous American architecture to the California landscape, creating a unique aesthetic and an innovative building system.

Like the pre-Columbians, Wright drew his California forms from the earth, but his technological innovations were new. He sculpted exotic shelters from hillsides and wove them with steel and glass to create open, inspiring spaces for modern living. His California legacy was based on his principles of organic architecture, in which a building grows from the site, the client's needs, and the inherent nature of the materials. His modular building schemes, pure geometric forms, and integral ornament had been tried before, but their expression here was driven by a quest for new directions and increased simplicity.

The primitive forms that Wright called on during the decade 1917–27 gave rise to doors and windows that looked like those of pre-Columbian temples. His crisp, sculptural handling of the plaster at Hollyhock house (1921) gave it the appearance of stone.

THE TEXTILE-BLOCK SYSTEM

TECHNOLOGY FOR THE GOLDEN STATE

THE FOCUS OF WRIGHT'S INVENTIVENESS in California was a standardized building method using concrete block, a popular material. Wright had long been fascinated by concrete, which was cheaper than stone and could be manipulated. He devised an interlocking system of precast-concrete blocks, called textile blocks, that were interwoven with steel. Back-to-back precast blocks served as structural elements, not merely ornament.

Molds in various patterns were created, and then blocks mixing local aggregate, cement, and water were cast on the site. The textile-block walls had a hollow interior space, but steel reinforcing rods were inserted in channels between the blocks and filled with grout.

The structures synthesized primitive architectural forms, Wright's childhood training with Froebel blocks, and new building technologies. He believed that the system would be inexpensive, easy to build without skilled labor, fireproof, and flexible. Unfortunately, construction difficulties and moisture problems precluded more than four textile-block houses, but Wright's interest in concrete block remained strong.

▦ A certain simple technique, larger in organization but no more complex in execution than that of rug weaving, builds the building. ▦

Frank Lloyd Wright
Architectural Record, 1927

Concrete blocks in a symmetrical cross design for the Millard house (1923) (opposite) were massed to create walls unlike Wright's earlier, individualized decorative details for Midway Gardens (1913), the German Warehouse (1915), the Bogk house (1916), and Hollyhock house (1921). A totally different design (left) was used for the Freeman house (1923).

The intricately patterned blocks of the Ennis house (1923) created dramatic, textured architectural forms on a Los Angeles hillside. Wright used simpler concrete blocks for the Lloyd Jones house (1929) in Tulsa, Oklahoma, and his Usonian Automatic houses of the 1950s.

WRIGHT'S APPRENTICES

The simple textile-block concept created rhythmic columns but complex construction problems at the Storer house (1923). Wright opened a small Los Angeles office with his son Lloyd to try to strengthen their client base but gave it little attention.

IN THE EARLY 1920S WRIGHT PERIODICALLY stopped in California on his way to and from Japan to discuss plans for Hollyhock house and the Barnsdall complex, the first of his Los Angeles commissions. His long absences had drawn his oldest son, Lloyd, into the project in 1919, when Wright asked him to find a contractor and landscape the house. An able designer at age twenty-nine, Lloyd had trained with the landscape architects Olmsted and Olmsted and later worked for the California architect Irving Gill, a pioneer in concrete.

Lloyd did some renderings but sent most of the drafting to Rudolph M. Schindler, who was at Taliesin in 1918–21. Schindler, an Austrian immigrant, eventually went to California to oversee construction of Hollyhock house. Later, in practice for himself, he helped the owner, Aline Barnsdall, with various details of her properties and did additional designs for Samuel and Harriet Freeman.

Completion of the problematic textile-block houses was left to Lloyd. The frustrated son was soon forced to assume the added role of arbitrator and construction supervisor.

1915–22 Wright travels to Tokyo twelve times to work on the Imperial Hotel (completed **1923**) and other commissions

1915 The movie industry begins

1916 Negotiations open for Aline Barnsdall's Hollyhock house

1917 The De Stijl art movement is founded in Holland

1918 World War I ends

1919 Prohibition begins

1920s The modern movement sweeps Europe and infiltrates American architecture

1920–21 Construction begins on Barnsdall's Hollyhock house and residences A and B

1923 Wright opens an office in West Hollywood with his son Lloyd; the Millard house in Pasadena is designed (completed 1924)

1923 Wright's mother dies, and he divorces Catherine and marries Miriam Noel; the Imperial Hotel survives an earthquake

1924 Wright returns to Chicago and meets Olgivanna Hinzenberg

1924 Barnsdall offers Hollyhock house to the City of Los Angeles (accepted 1926)

1924–26 Construction of the Storer, Freeman, and Ennis houses is supervised by Lloyd

1925 Wright's work is published by Wendingen in Germany; a second fire burns Taliesin; Iovanna, Wright's seventh child, is born

1926 The bank takes title to Taliesin; Wright begins *An Autobiography*

1927 Wright codesigns the Arizona Biltmore Hotel, using his textile-block system

1927 Miriam Noel and Wright are divorced after a three-year separation; Wright returns to Taliesin

1928 Wright marries Olgivanna and forms Frank Lloyd Wright, Inc., to give himself a new start

1929 Wright designs a textile-block house in Oklahoma for his cousin Richard Lloyd Jones

1950s Some of Wright's earlier textile-block technology is used for his Usonian Automatic houses

Clockwise from top left: Wright's first wife, Catherine; client Aline Barnsdall with her daughter, Sugar Top; second wife Miriam Noel; and third wife Olgivanna, with their daughter, Iovanna.

Unique modular construction system

Technology used to enhance the designs structurally and visually

Concrete or concretelike materials

Wright's interest in concrete manifested in cast blocks of varying patterns as well as in stucco

Primitive forms recalling pre-Columbian dwellings

Emphasis on rectilinear geometric lines, flat roofs, battered walls, and heavy massing

Dramatic contrasts

The solidity of concrete vs. the openness of glass; light vs. dark; compressed vs. released spaces

Integral ornament

Raised textile-block surfaces used to create rich textures

Hillside siting

Buildings embracing the landscape to create dramatic views while partially concealing themselves

More enclosures, less openness

Protected shelters and secretiveness through use of corridors, nooks, crannies, and overlooks

Cavelike interiors

Closed off from the street, with a large vertical fireplace at the core

Informal, vertical plans

Stacked rooms and unconventional placement of spaces, reflecting the clients' independent natures and casual lifestyles

Dining rooms in transition

Spaces on a different level from the living room

Large expanses of glass

Most often vertical rather than horizontal light screens as in the Prairie Style period

Little art glass

The last examples of Wright's famous geometric patterns

Minimal custom furniture

Lack of time to complete interior furnishing details

Difficult client relationships

Many conflicts and communication problems, with projects left to his son Lloyd and others to complete

Clockwise from top left: Varied ways of stacking the Ennis house block pattern, even upside down. The Storer house, whose motif was combined with large areas of plain block for contrast.

BARNSDALL (HOLLYHOCK) HOUSE

HOLLYWOOD, CALIFORNIA. 1919-21

Decorative arts at Hollyhock house include integral design features such as cast stone, abstract hollyhock columns, and art glass windows, as well as inset Japanese screens and Wright-designed furniture.

ECCENTRIC AND RESTLESS, THE OIL heiress Aline Barnsdall met Wright in Chicago in 1916 and soon began discussing her dream of an experimental theater featuring indigenous American themes and talent. She was attracted to Wright's efforts to create an indigenous architecture and soon engaged him to execute a complete arts compound in Los Angeles with theaters, shops, and residences for her artists and herself.

By 1919, when she purchased a thirty-six-acre tract, Wright was heavily involved in his work on the Imperial Hotel in Japan. Both client and architect were constantly traveling. Construction of the first building in the complex—her own home, Hollyhock house (named for her favorite flower)—finally began in 1920.

In a transitional stage, Wright was seeking a new architectural vocabulary. His interest in the "primitive abstractions of man's nature—ancient arts of the Maya, the Inca, the Toltec" is reflected in designs such as this. Built of hollow terra-cotta tile walls and wood framing covered with stucco, the residence used art stone ornament in a mix of cement, granite, and gravel. Stylized

From the cloisterlike front entry (right), the house provides a wealth of design experiences (opposite, clockwise from top left): a bridge over the courtyard, a panoramic prospect of the valley, views of lush greenery, and art glass windows in the nursery.

⸬ Stately and yet endearing, even playful, the house is all at once an oasis, paradise garden, rooftop promenade, lookout and retreat. It is also a theater for the performance each day of sun and shadow, a place of peculiar enchantment. ⸬

Donald Hoffmann
Frank Lloyd Wright's
Hollyhock House, 1992

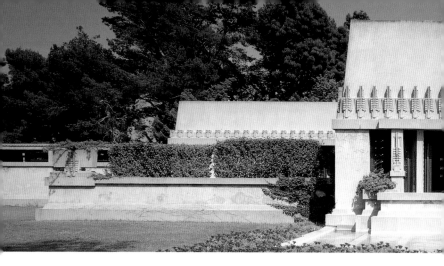

Hollyhock house embraces the crest of Olive Hill, using forms reminiscent of the earth-born architecture of the Mayans (above). Its battered walls, flat roofs, simple bands of geometric ornament, and inward orientation all encourage comparison with Amerindian ruins uncovered early in the century.

hollyhock designs were cast and grouped into linear friezes, used singly on posts and columns, paired on urns, and displayed as finials on the roof. Unlike the other California houses of the 1920s, Hollyhock house was never intended to be built of concrete. It used concrete for ornament only, yet its design is restrained and monolithic.

The house is entered through a typically hidden entrance leading to a loggia that opens to a central garden court with a pool. To the right, an enchanting living room provides an oasis from the sun. Its fireplace is an altar incorporating earth, air, fire, and water. The arms

of the U-shaped house hold dining and kitchen spaces on the north side and bedrooms and a library on the south. The complex plan is interwoven with delights: connecting passageways, pergolas, level changes, and curious nooks contrasting with grand rooftop overlooks.

Barnsdall lost interest in the house before it was finished, leaving art glass and furniture incomplete. She lived there only briefly before donating the property to the City of Los Angeles, which now administers it as a museum. Wright designed some forty-five buildings for her, but only her home and residence A and B were executed.

The living room's abstract art stone mantelpiece (page 26) ties together all geometric forms used in the house. A skylight overhead reflects light into a gold-lined pool. Custom furniture created for the living areas (page 27) was augmented by wood banding connecting the elements.

MILLARD HOUSE (LA MINIATURA)

THE FIRST OF WRIGHT'S FOUR TEXTILE-block houses was designed for another artistic, idealistic, and intellectual woman whom Wright knew from Chicago. His former clients Alice and George Millard had built a 1906 Prairie Style house in Highland Park, Illinois, before moving to Pasadena, where George died in 1918. They were rare-book dealers and collectors who had expanded into antiques and imported decorative arts.

Wright was enthusiastic about his new concrete-block building system and encouraged Alice Millard to try it. Standardized blocks were assembled in pairs, a patterned one outside, a smooth one inside, with an air space in between. In this first execution, however, the blocks had no metal reinforcing rods and were set using a conventional mortar bed with an expanded diamond-mesh metal lath. Although the blocks became the interior wall surface of all perimeter walls, other walls were plastered; ceilings were wood and plaster, and some floors were wood.

The primary block design, a symmetrical cross, was pierced and sectioned to serve various needs and

The house is entered from beneath a bridge between the main building and the garage or from a path along the reflecting pool at the lower dining room level. Its ravine location was unique for Wright—hillside sites were much more common for him.

combined with plain ones to create new patterns. Other geometric designs were massed inside, rising like ancient walls of carved stone. A skeletal concrete frame holds the elements together, and tall piers of rectangular blocks express the structure. At night light filters through the cross-shaped openings like stars in the sky.

A treasure box, the house is nestled in the flora and fauna of a ravine. Stacking the rooms vertically, Wright provided opportunities for overlooks from the rooftop terrace on down. Balconies open up the two-story living room on the primary middle level. The three bedrooms are stacked on the north side, one on each level. A large central chimney mass inside creates a castlelike solidity. The changing levels and textures, the laciness of some walls, and the monolithic power of others create a mood that is exotic and mysterious.

Although the experimental construction method created problems for the architect and builder, particularly in getting uniform blocks from the wooden molds, it was an ideal retreat that served as a perfect background for the collections of this adventuresome client.

An ideal was realized in the Millard house. Though technically primitive in view of improvements in the block system that were on the horizon, formally it is the most perfect of the block houses built on the West Coast.

Robert L. Sweeney
Wright in Hollywood, 1994

The balcony of the main bedroom (opposite) offers a treetop overlook.

Inside, smooth blocks make a suitable background for paintings in the dining room (page 32), while pierced ones allow light to filter in and enhance the living room (page 33).

STORER HOUSE

LIKE WRIGHT, DR. JOHN STORER, A homeopathic doctor, had come from Chicago and was enticed by California's real estate opportunities. Before both became disillusioned, they built a curious sand castle in the Hollywood foothills. Wright adapted an unbuilt design for the Charles Lowes (1922) for his new textile-block system.

He changed the construction process to eliminate mortar and strengthen the building by adding steel rods in the block walls. Hoping to avoid the uneven blocks encountered at the Millard house, Wright had metal molds machine made and used greater pressure and longer curing times for the blocks. Under Lloyd Wright's supervision, the same system was used in the Freeman and Ennis houses, built nearly simultaneously. Wright had hoped both to eliminate the mason and to patent the system.

Eleven block patterns were interwoven in various combinations, creating changing textures inside and outside this vertical composition on a steep hillside. Two-story columns of glass alternate with the blocks to allow views of the ocean and the city beyond.

Rows of block-covered piers rise from a platform to support the house's wood beams and joists. Cost overruns on the project, incurred as Wright sought to improve the textile-block houses, were enormous. John Storer died bankrupt in 1927.

The living area on the second floor, above the dining room, has terraces on both sides. Bedrooms are stacked two over two in the west wing. The kitchen and servant areas adjoin the dining room on the main floor, where the entrance, obscured by windows, opens quietly into the space. Terraces with a pool and planters surround the house, their walls meandering along the hillside, retaining the earth, and defining pathways.

The blocks' versatility can be seen inside. The solidity of the peripheral walls, the altarlike strength of the chimney, the rhythm of the pillars, the filigree of the pierced blocks, their coolness opposed to the warmth of wood and sunshine, all add enchantment. Windows that continue beyond the ceiling release the cubic quality of the spaces, yet the plan is less fluid than Wright's Prairie houses of the previous decade—moving up and down more than side to side.

Occupied by Storer only from 1924 to 1927, the house was rented in 1931 by Rudolph Schindler's wife, who helped improve its condition. Lloyd Wright's son Eric recently supervised a complete restoration.

Shadows add drama to the square-within-a-square patterns (opposite and above).

Wright's son Lloyd, who oversaw the original construction, designed the landscaping (page 38) as well as colorful geometric awnings for the upper terraces (page 39).

Uniquely located on the top level of the house, above the dining room, the living room is a towerlike retreat from the more sociable spaces below. The solid chimney core, set off-center, grounds this aerie surrounded by art glass windows and doors.

FREEMAN HOUSE

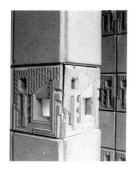

A terrace in back, on the hillside elevation (opposite), is accessible from both bedrooms. Looking back toward it, the drama of the corner windows—designed without piers—becomes apparent. The intricate block pattern (above) is believed to be an abstraction of the site's flora.

THE SMALLEST OF THE TEXTILE-BLOCK houses was designed for Samuel and Harriet Freeman, a young salesman and a progressive, independent dancer who remained in the house for sixty years. In this compact but dramatic design, Wright used the cantilever to open spaces to panoramic views of the lush landscape and Hollywood beyond.

Seen from the street, it is a simple one-story, semiclosed building. Inside, the house opens to a spacious central room, uninterrupted by support piers. The outer wall is mostly glass, which fluidly wraps around corners to demonstrate the building's structural freedom. More glass is placed in pierced concrete blocks to further contrast solids and voids. Two large concrete support beams span the living space. The wood roof and floors are cantilevered from a series of block piers that tie the building to the steep, south-sloping hillside. The house is alive with the play of light and shadow.

The living area's openness is transformed into a cavelike intimacy on the fireplace wall. Wright designed high-back benches to create an inglenook around the

massive chimney of concrete blocks. Several years later, Wright's former apprentice Rudolph Schindler designed more comfortable seating there to encourage informal gathering at the hearth. The private sleeping areas are on the floor below, both levels extended through the use of terraces.

The principal block pattern, one of fifty-two variations, is similar to a design carved in stone for Wright's Imperial Hotel (1915–23) in Tokyo. The intricate, geometric composition introduced a diagonal counterpoint to the cubic structure. One hundred a day were cast by hand, one at a time, in an 18-by-18-by-5-inch aluminum mold, and then cured for three weeks. The complex manipulations, combinations, and rotations of the various blocks, many plain, created new patterns and textures.

Construction costs totaled nearly $22,000—250 percent of Wright's estimate. Schindler later carried out modifications for the Freemans, including reconfiguring rooms on the lower level to create an apartment and a larger bedroom. He also designed many ingenious, compact cabinets that improved efficiency and livability.

Window walls (opposite) are supported by set-back piers like one above, which create a subtle division of space.

The living-dining area (pages 46–47) breaks from traditional, distinct dining rooms, reflecting changing social attitudes and previewing Wright's Usonian houses of the 1930s.

E N N I S   H O U S E

THE GRANDEST OF THE TEXTILE-BLOCK houses was the last and closest in appearance to pre-Columbian forms. Charles and Mabel Ennis, successful haberdashers, were said to be admirers of Mayan culture. Their half-acre lot was a knob in the foothills of the Santa Monica Mountains and offered spectacular views of the city. Because of its extended retaining walls of matching concrete blocks, the monumental building with battered walls seems even larger and more archaeological. A large motor courtyard and more block walls join the residence to a garage and caretakers quarters.

Despite its size, the house has few rooms. All living spaces are on different levels of the main floor and are connected by a dramatic one-hundred-foot-long colonnade. Terraces and gardens further extend the grand spaces.

Wright's use of offset blocks, overhead blocks, and telescoping forms completed his experiments with the textile-block structural system. More than twenty variations of the master pattern were mixed with solid blocks to define form, used in rows to build parapet

▓ The Ennis opus is an extraordinary blend of wonderful interior spaces placed on a site that posed, in the first instance, the problem of retaining ground and building intact. ▓

Bruce Brooks Pfeiffer
Frank Lloyd Wright: Monographs. 1914–1923, 1985

The archaeological shapes of the Ennis house rise from the steep hillside site and can be seen from miles away. Careful engineering was required to anchor the building, terraces, and retaining walls to the hill.

walls, massed to create a textured wall, and stacked to form columns. The massing is the most intricate and multidimensional of all the California houses.

The interiors, however, were not completed according to Wright's specifications. Art glass windows similar to early Wright designs for his Prairie houses are incompatible with the concrete block. So many modifications were made by the owners during construction that Wright withdrew from the project. With their contractor's help, wood ceiling details were changed, marble was used instead of slate for the colonnade floor, and ironwork by a local artisan introduced incongruous, Hispanic-style curvilinear forms. The golden fireplace mosaic, however, was similar to earlier ones in Wright's Husser house (1899) in Chicago and Darwin Martin house (1904) in Buffalo, New York.

Wright provided revised plans with furniture designs for a new owner in the 1940s, but they were not completed. The house, now owned by a foundation, stands as a symbol of Wright's California decade—grand in vision but problematic in execution.

A long colonnade (opposite) connects the living spaces. Throughout the house Prairie-style art glass windows and doors (above) are some of Wright's last such designs. Looking to more progressive methods of manipulating glass, he abandoned this old but labor-intensive craft.

Located in the grand connecting loggia opposite the living area, the fireplace is celebrated with a golden glass wisteria mosaic (right and opposite). The dining room is to the left, up the stairs—setting it apart but not isolated from the living area.

The connecting colonnade opens outside as well (pages 54–55), providing a shaded area adjoining the garden. A pool there is well protected from the street by a retaining wall. Alternating bands of solid and patterned blocks accent the dominant horizontality of Wright's design.

Alofsin, Anthony. *Frank Lloyd Wright: The Lost Years, 1910–1922.* Chicago: University of Chicago Press, 1993.

Dunham, Judith. *Details of Frank Lloyd Wright: The California Work, 1909–1974.* San Francisco: Chronicle, 1994.

Gebhard, David. *Romanza: The California Architecture of Frank Lloyd Wright.* San Francisco: Chronicle, 1988.

Hoffmann, Donald. *Frank Lloyd Wright's Hollyhock House.* New York: Dover Publications, 1992.

Pfeiffer, Bruce Brooks, ed. *Frank Lloyd Wright: Monographs. 1914–1923.* Vol. 4. Tokyo: ADA Edita, 1985.

Secrest, Meryle. *Frank Lloyd Wright: A Biography.* New York: Knopf, 1992.

Smith, Kathryn. *Frank Lloyd Wright: Hollyhock House and Olive Hill.* New York: Rizzoli, 1992.

Sweeney, Robert L. *Wright in Hollywood.* Architectural History Foundation. Cambridge: MIT Press, 1994.

Wright, Frank Lloyd. *Frank Lloyd Wright: Collected Writings.* Vols. 1–2. Edited by Bruce Brooks Pfeiffer. New York: Rizzoli, 1992.

The author wishes to thank Jeffrey M. Chusid, Virginia Kazor, Bruce Brooks Pfeiffer, Kathryn Smith, and Robert L. Sweeney for their scholarship and assistance. She also acknowledges the owners of these buildings for their cooperation and stewardship.